T0128422

I CAN'T SAVE YOUR MARRIAGE, but You Can!

WHY MARRIAGES COLLAPSE AND HOW TO MOVE
FORWARD AND RESTORE YOUR MARRIAGE.
TEN REAL LIFE COUNSELING SESSIONS INCLUDED!

NORMAN BISHOP

WESTBOW
PRESS®
A DIVISION OF THOMAS NELSON
& ZONDERVAN

WestBow Press books may be ordered through booksellers or by contacting:

WestBow Press
A Division of Thomas Nelson & Zondervan
1663 Liberty Drive
Bloomington, IN 47403
www.westbowpress.com
844-714-3454

Because of the dynamic nature of the Internet, any web addresses or
links contained in this book may have changed since publication and
may no longer be valid. The views expressed in this work are solely those
of the author and do not necessarily reflect the views of the publisher,
and the publisher hereby disclaims any responsibility for them.

Any people depicted in stock imagery provided by Getty Images are
models, and such images are being used for illustrative purposes only.
Certain stock imagery © Getty Images.

ISBN: 978-1-6642-8241-4 (sc)
ISBN: 978-1-6642-8242-1 (hc)
ISBN: 978-1-6642-8240-7 (e)

Library of Congress Control Number: 2022919984

Print information available on the last page.

WestBow Press rev. date: 12/02/2022

Contents

Dedication

I am grateful to my Lord and Savior Jesus Christ for taking me on this journey called life. Through all the trials and tests, You have never abandoned me. I honor You for allowing me to be transparent and for the wisdom you have given me to author this book.

I dedicate this book to my wife, Rochelle, who has been steadfast in her love for her husband. I also dedicate this book to our three, adult children, Andrea, Maurice, and Marcus. This book could not have been written without you! You guys make me so proud! I dedicate this book to my dad who demonstrated how a man ought to be and live. I honor my late mother for her courage and love towards me. It was a joy to take care of my mother. Finally, I honor my sister, Gwen Jackson, for our strong bond, and to my brother-n-law Arthur Jackson Sr.

Acknowledgements

I had three pastors in my life, and I want to acknowledge all three. The Bible says to much is given; much will be required. Luke 12:48. I have been given much by the late Pastor Benjamin Smith, Dr. Wesley Pinnock, and Bishop Eric Lambert. These men of God instilled in me a strong commitment to Christ, a strong commitment to prayer, a strong commitment to family, and a strong commitment to serve. I honor them today for their godly example not only to me but to the Body of Christ.

Preface

Norman Bishop was born and raised in Philadelphia, Pa. His parents separated early in life, and his mother spent five years in a mental facility. Because of that, Norman lived with his beloved Grand mother, Alma Bishop, for five years along with his sister, Gwen. As a teenager, Norman attended a boarding school where he saw firsthand the regular use of drugs and alcohol and was amazed seeing a student shooting up as a ninth grader. There were fights every day. What saved Norman through this torture, he could play basketball very well. Norman made the varsity team as a freshman and average twenty-five points on the junior varsity basketball team. The local newspaper mentioned him for his outstanding games. After high school, he attended Tuskegee University. Norman was shocked when he realized he could not do the work. He was not prepared for college work, and it showed in his GPA of 1.7. Because of his low-grade point average, he was not eligible to play varsity basketball. Norman was on probation with the intent to dismiss if he did not improve his average. More than any, Norman did not want to come back to Philly a failure! He worked extremely hard and push his GPA to 2.5. As a freshman, Norman was close to two Christians, Mike and Allen, and he wasn't a Christian. They let him in their circle and accepted Norman with all his rough habits. They lived in Atlanta, Ga. They would see the Atlanta Hawks play. Mike's Father was a pastor, so Norman had to attend Sunday services. Since Norman stayed for free and ate all that southern food, church on Sunday was no big deal. Norman made it through his first year, barely!

It was good being back home for the summer. Norman worked through the summer and enjoyed playing basketball and tennis. One night he was taking a friend to the Philadelphia 76er's game. As he was walking, still on his block, a guy pulled a gun on him and said, "Give me your coat!" His leather coat was brand new, and he did not want to give it to him. Norman wanted to take his gun. "Perhaps, it wasn't real," he thought. However, he decided my life was more valuable than the coat, so he slowly begin to take off his coat. Suddenly, two cop cars pulled on my block and raided a house near where they were. The guy threw the gun in the bushes and took off, and Norman was in shock. What just happened? He could have shot and killed Norman. It was right there on his block that a scripture came to his mind. It said, what shall it profit a man if he gains the whole world and lose his soul. Mark 8:36. This was a scripture Norman learned as an 11-year-old at Neighborhood Bible Club. He stopped going at age 13 and never went to church on a regular basis or picked up a Bible again until after this incident. Yet, Norman remembered this scripture as a 19-year-old. He concluded that if there was a hell he was going there. With no one around, Norman gave his heart, and his life to Jesus Christ and never looked back. Jesus rescued his life!

When Norman went back to Tuskegee University for his second year, his friends, especially Mike and Allen, notice the change immediately. Other said, "Bishop, once you see all the new freshman girls, you will be back to your old self again." However, that was not the case. Norman wanted to live for Christ, and it showed even after he graduated. Yes, he graduated! Norman even made the dean's list his junior and senior year! Plus, he made the tennis team his senior year. In 1977, Norman graduated with his BA Degree in English and minor in economics.

Norman graduated from Deliverance Bible Institute after taking twenty Bible classes. He received his teaching certificate from the Evangelical Teachers Training Association. The director asked him to teach English and other Bible classes at Deliverance Bible institute. He taught there for twenty years and served as a deacon for ten years. Norman continued to conduct pre-marriage and marriage advising at

True Light Fellowship Church. He taught classes at their Bible school and preached his first sermon there.

Norman was asked to pastor two churches. He chose neither one. It is not about what Norman wanted, but what God wanted. He joined Bethel Deliverance International Church and began to train leaders at Bethel along with leaders from twenty-five other churches. What an honor! Norman was part of the Pastoral Staff where he continued with pre marriage and marriage advising. In 2012, Norman attended Liberty University and received his master's degree in Pastoral Counseling in 2014. He graduated with a 3.5 grade point average while working a full-time job, working in ministry, and taking care of his family, which always have been a priority! One must not be a public success and a private failure. One must not give the appearance of a successful home when there is strife, division, and a lack of direction and love.

After completing over two hundred advising and counseling sessions without charge, Norman felt impressed to author this book. Yes, through all the counseling sessions and wedding performed, he never charged anyone a fee! His goal was to help couples have a good foundation and to help married couples have a stronger marriage and a stronger family. The goal of this book is to give spiritual and practical advice concerning their marriage and their family. This book will help you! Read it repeatedly and apply the principles in this book. Your family is at stake! I can't save your marriage, but you can!

Introduction

We are about to begin our journey. The success of your marriage and your family does not depend on God, your pastor, or this book; it depends on you! Therefore, take ownership of that! If your marriage fails, it is because of you. Don't blame your spouse. Don't blame your children. Don't blame your job or your church. Blame yourself! When one blames others, it shifts the blame off you and places it on someone or something else. That will not work, and failure will occur. Remember, it is easier to blame others than ourselves. Look in the mirror and ask yourself, "Where have I gone wrong?" Not where my spouse or children have gone wrong, but where have I gone wrong? If you will honestly ask yourself that question, you are headed in the right direction!

I have concluded after two hundred plus sessions over a forty-year period that I can't save anyone's marriage. As a young minister, I thought it was my job to save struggling marriages and prevent newly weds from separating or divorcing. There is no amount of money, babies, sermons, or books that can save your marriage if one wants out. This book is a tool filled with spiritual and practical advice along with 40 years of marriage to assist you in saving your marriage. However, you must do the work.

I saw couples before they were married and couples after they were married. Some couples were married for 3 months and others for 20 years. I will share several sessions without giving any names. I am proud to be known as a person who believes in confidentiality and practice that. The goal of this book is to give spiritual and practical principles in making your marriage strong and to assist in saving your marriage. Remember, I can't save your marriage, but you can.

Chapter One

A SOLID FOUNDATION

Build your marriage on a solid foundation.
Matthew 7:24-27

When one begins to build a home, the construction company makes sure that the ground is good to build on. If the ground is bad, the inspectors will not approve the ground. It would save the couple money and frustration if they knew the ground was bad. Therefore, spend time investigating the ground. Investigate the person you want to marry. Yes, I said investigate! How is their ground? When one applies for a job, doesn't one investigate to see if the company is solvent or in bankruptcy? Doesn't one investigate the turnover rate and benefits? The job will surely spend time investigating future employees. They look at credit reports. They will look at employment history and talk to present and past coworkers. What are you looking at? You may not even consider this part, and we are just getting started. In my experience, couples are looking at the wrong things. My future spouse has all the outward features that I am looking for! I love their smile. I love the way they make me feel. They really care about me. This can go on and on. I have three questions for you. First, are they a Christian? Second, how do you know? Third, what fruit do you see manifested in their daily life? One cannot build on bad ground. The house will collapse. Do not build your marriage on looks, money, or feeling. Build your marriage on godly principles! If you are planning a marriage with one who is not a Christian, you are building on a weak foundation and your marriage will collapse. How can two walk together unless they are agreed? Amos 3:3. One spouse wants to go to the night club, and the other wants to go to church. Each is going in a different direction. This is not the way to start any marriage. One must build on a solid foundation. A bridge foundation goes deep into the ground to support to the bridge. It must be able to withstand the cars, trucks, and intense winds. Likewise, your marriage must be able to withstand intense winds of unemployment, disagreements, financial issues, health issues, and family issues. Without a solid foundation, marriages collapse. Why did you marry this person? There are over one hundred reasons why people get married. Some people get married because they are lonely, because she's attractive, because he's handsome, because of age, because of pregnancy, because of money, or because of parents' rules in the home. I'm sure you can think of reasons yourself. The problem is when one marries for the wrong reasons, the foundation is weak. The weight of life challenges will cause the marriage to collapse. A marriage built on a solid foundation in most cases will be able to weather life challenges. Matthew 7:24-27 tells us to build on a solid foundation. It starts with the Word of God and layered with love. That's a foundation!

Discussion Questions:

1. Have you really investigated the person you plan to marry?

2. What is their job history?

3. How does your future spouse treat their parents?

4. What is their credit score?

5. How much debt does your future spouse have?

Chapter Two

REASONS FOR GETTING MARRIED

Love is patient, Love is kind. It does not envy, it does not boast, it is not proud. It does not dishonor others: it is not self-seeking. It is not easily angered; it keeps no record of wrong!
1 Corinthians 13:4-5 NIV

You need to read these two verses at least five times right now then at least once per day! Now, do you really want to get married? Have you counted the cost? Do you really know the person you plan to spend the rest of your life with? Are you friends? Friendship speaks of mutual respect, mutual love, and mutual commitment. It cannot be just one showing respect, love, and commitment. It must be both. Do their actions show these three qualities each day? It is not a one-time event. See, the person you marry will not be the same in ten years. Therefore, you must keep your eyes open and not fall for all the glitter. All the glitter is not gold. Are you patient and kind to each other? Do you have frequent, intense arguments, and disagreements? Does one always want their way without considering what the other wants or need? Love doesn't easily fly off the handle but willingly forgives and make corrections! Love keeps no record of wrong. Why would a husband or a wife hold bitterness towards their spouse for something that happened twenty years ago? Through the power of the Holy Spirit and the willingness to forgive, the chains of bitterness can be broken. Honorable deeds will not break the chains of bitterness. Ephesians 4:31-32 NIV tells us to get rid of all bitterness, rage, anger, brawling, and slander, along with every form of malice. Be kind and compassionate to each other, forgiving each other, just as in Christ, God forgave you. Are you bitter against your spouse? It will not go away by will power or by ignoring it. You must own up to it, confess it, and ask the Lord for help in forgiving your spouse. My friend, it is hard but easier when we yield to the Holy Spirit. Bitterness can bring sickness to our bodies. We must not hold all that negative junk inside. God set us free with the freedom to enjoy our lives and not be bound in chains of bitterness, regrets, or scars from our past. If the Son has set you free, you really will be free! St. John 8:36 CSB.

One should never have to wonder if their partner really loves them. When I say partner, I am talking about a man and a woman. Love must be expressive and show that they care. Remember, you must watch the actions of the one you plan to marry. Are they saved and demonstrate that commitment to Christ? It is not a perfect life but a genuine and sincere life. We must never depend on our partner to make us whole or to make us happy. Happiness is only temporary anyway. One can be happy one day and sad the next day. However, God gives His children joy, which speaks on inner gladness. Even when I had a car accident, I was not happy about that, but I still had joy! The joy that God gives is eternal regardless of the present situation. That makes me happy! When our water was shut off for non-payment, I was not happy about that. I am just being transparent with you. However, I still had joy down in my soul and happy that my wife did not leave me! She showed considerable patience and care. Forty years later, she continues to show patience and care and yes, it goes both ways.

As you read this book, I am not giving you just theory but forty years of marriage experience, and I am not afraid to share the challenges that comes with being married. Marriage is not a fairy tale where your knight in shining armor comes to take you out the ghetto. Marriage brings reality. It brings real life to the forefront.

Now, let's look at some reasons why people get married. If I asked you, what your reason for getting married? What would you tell me? I'm sure love would be near the top. However, one cannot live on love. I heard a preacher say that love without finance is nonsense. That was funny and correct. I remember a couple telling me that they were going to live off love. Neither had a job but would be staying with one of the parents. I am sure you can think of reasons why people get married. Here are some reasons:

1. *Age - I would like to get married before I'm fifty.*
2. *Loneliness - I need a companion.*
3. *Children - I want someone to help me with my children.*
4. *Pregnant -Marriage will hide my pregnancy, so I won't feel ashamed.*
5. *Family – I don't want to obey my parent's rules.*
6. *Sexual Intercourse – I want to have sex without feeling guilty.*
7. *Housekeeper – I need someone to cook and clean*
8. *Financial Support – I need someone with plenty of money.*
9. *Gifts – I want nice gifts.*
10. *Physical attraction – She is beautiful! He is a body builder!*
11. *Best friends got married – I don't want to feel left out.*
12. *Fulfil God's purpose – I want my marriage to bring God glory.*
13. *Arranged marriage – Parents pick my marriage partner.*
14. *Biological clock – I want a baby now!*
15. *Wedding – I want a large and beautiful wedding.*

Of course, there are more reasons. However, if one marries for all the wrong reasons, the foundation is weak. It was built on unstable ground and will collapse. Just as it takes time to build a house, it takes time to build a solid friendship. There is a TV show titled, Love at first sight. I don't subscribe to that. My understanding is that they are not friends and don't even know each other. Marriage is hard enough even when you are friends and know each other. Marriage is work! Married people lose their jobs too, and the bills keep on coming. Married people have children who needs care. What about college when the time comes? Please, don't imagine after the wedding that you will live happily ever after. Life has challenges!

When a man and a woman stand before the minister to be married, do you believe they are thinking that they will be divorce or separated in six months to a year? Who thinks like that on their special day? I would guess not too many. Unfortunately, many marriages end in divorce or separation and the church is not exempt from divorce or separation either. There are fifty or more reasons why people get divorce. It could be abuse, drugs, alcohol, too young, financial, non-caring, meanness, no communication, or no affection. Understand that professional athletes as well as celebrities get divorce. Millionaires and billionaires get divorce also. No one is immune to divorce. What is the problem? As you read on, we will talk about that more in details.

Review Questions:

1. Find ten reasons why people get married that are not on this list. Do not move forward without finding ten!

2. When was the last time you showed patience and kindness to your spouse or future spouse?

3. Give two honest reasons why you want to marry your future spouse?

4. Why do you think some millionaires marry more than once?

5. What can you do to prevent separation and divorce in your marriage?

Chapter Three

ARE YOU A GOOD LISTENER?

A wise person will listen and follow instruction.
Proverbs 9:9 NIV

*In all my counseling years, I have discovered that some just don't listen.
A wise person will listen and increase learning. The meek will He guide
in judgment or the decision-making process. Psalms 25:9. However, the
prideful and the know it all come to the counseling sessions to enlighten
the counselor. They already have the date of their marriage prepared,
with their honeymoon prepared, and invitations ready to be mailed.
They have not even had one counseling session! What's the use in giving
counsel when the couple have already put out thousands of dollars!
Why would they listen to any counselor who sees danger signs? Pride
and so call love cause one to be blinded by the reality that confronts
them. Even if they do not agree with the counselor, why not consider
what the counselor instructs? How many times have I heard the phrase
if I only had listened? Many heartaches and struggles could have been
avoided just by listening. Many have lost their lives needlessly if they*

had only listened. Don't drink and drive. Don't jog alone. Get a check up regularly. Whether you are getting married, or need some directions in your marriage, then listen to your counselor. Your counselor is there to help you, not to hurt you. I remember one session where I saw too many danger signs. The gentleman wanted to take his future wife back to his homeland in Africa and start a new life away from her children and her family. This was one of many danger signs. God wants the family to be strong and united, not weak and divided. They were so confident that they were right, and I was wrong that what I said went in one ear and out the other. They did not consider what I said. It was incredibly sad to me, because I cared about them like all couples and wanted the best for them. They got married, but I outlined the dangers signs that I saw. In less than two years, she was back in the states, divorce, no money, and no place to live. Her family did not forget how she left her kids and her family to be with someone she only knew for a few months. I have a question for you. Do you need a man or a woman so bad that you are willing to separate from your children and family to be with someone who says I love you? The blessing of the Lord makes rich, and He adds no sorrow to it. Proverbs 10:22. The Lord wants your marriage to be strong and filled with love. However, it will not happen when we refuse to listen. James 1:19 GNT tells us to be quick to listen, not quick to act, but slow to speak, and slow to anger. We must be willing to give heed to sound instructions, so we can prosper. Proverbs 16:20. NIV

Another couple requested marriage counseling. I asked one question, "What is the problem?" They argued for one hour, back and forth, and I did not interrupt them! I listened. After the hour, I told them that they needed to get in the habit of listening to each other and stop playing the blame game. Each was blaming the other for the condition of their marriage. Both were to blame because both were unwilling to listen. I could not help them, because they refuse to listen to each other and refuse to listen to me. I want you to see how important listening is to a marriage. When we listen and give our spouse the undivided attention they deserve, it speaks volume. It says *that you are so important to me that I am willing to listen to you. It takes time to listen. We show our spouse that we love them when we are willing to take the time to listen. It doesn't mean that you must agree, but you must be willing to listen. I could not help this couple. The marriage ended in divorce.*

Discussion Questions:

1. Do you agree that the best way to have enjoyable conversation is to listen?

2. Explain the value of listening to your spouse or future spouse.

3. Share a time when you said, "If I only had listened."

4. What are some reasons for not listening to our spouse?

5. What steps can you take to improve your listening skills?

Chapter Four

THE JOY OF TEAMWORK

> *Above all, love each other earnestly, since love*
> *covers over a multitude of sins. Show hospitality*
> *to one another without grumbling.*
> *1 Peter 4:8-9 ESV*

Working together to reach certain goals is teamwork.

The Apostle Paul used the example of the human body to describe teamwork. I was a good basketball player making the varsity high school team as a freshman. I played little but on the junior varsity team, I average twenty-five points a game. I was a shooter. My shooting was what I brought to the team. Even as a senior in high school and beyond, it was my shooting that made our team successful. One year in the playoffs, I decided that I was going to lead the team in assists. What a mistake that was! Our team got destroyed! It was my fault! I refused to shoot but passed to others who were not good at shooting. They had other abilities. The point is I was out of position which caused my teammates to be out of position.

In our body, each member of the body has a specific function. Our eyes have a specific function. Our eyes don't try to hear. Our ears don't try to talk. I believe you get the picture. When parts of the body refuses to function in their own area, it is known as a cancer. It acts independently from the body. When each part of the body functions in unity, there is teamwork. My left hand in not jealous of my right hand even though I use it more. They are not in competition with each other.

As married couples, we need to be intentional about working as a team. What do you bring to the team or to the marriage? What will your spouse bring to the marriage? It will be hard for a marriage to be successful if one refuses to work as a team. Therefore, each must have the freedom to function in the area where they are gifted. I am the better cook than my wife. I am not just saying that. My wife would agree with that. However, she functions best in housekeeping and raising our three children, an excellent Mother. Our children are blessed because of her commitment to the family. Now that we are empty nesters, we can look back and see how the Lord helped us. Our children are blessed and successful in life because of our commitment in teaching and being an example before them. We chose to work as a team. Please don't get me wrong. We had plenty of arguments and disagreements. Come on, after 40 years of marriage, there will be challenges. However, we were able to work through our differences. Our foundation was strong. One must not give up because of a heated argument. Declare that divorce is not an option in our marriage. Be diligent in seeking to work things out! I guarantee you that you will look back on your marriage many years later and say, "I am so glad I did not quit on my marriage." How difference your life would be! May I say right here that physical abuse to a spouse and to the children is never acceptable! I do not see any biblical reason to stay with a spouse who is abusive mentally or physically. That is criminal and the police should be called! God has called us to peace not violence and abuse. I Corinthians 7:15. I understand that you love your spouse and want to keep the family together. However, you should love yourself and your children so much that you will protect them and yourself from harm.

The Bible tells us a house divided can not stand. Mark 3:25. It is important to stand together in your faith in Jesus Christ. It is not enough to go to church, sing on the choir, or even serve in areas in the church. Husbands and wives must have a personal relationship with the Lord Jesus Christ. I cannot emphasize that enough! Why would a Christian want to marry an unbeliever? Each of you are going in opposite directions. The Bible says, how can two walk together unless they agree? Amos 3:3. When one is not a Believer, they are being influenced by satan and their fleshly desires. The Believer is influenced by the Holy Spirit, the Word of God, and their fleshly desires also. That is why the pull of the flesh can cause a Believer to compromise and go against what they know is right. People tell me that their future spouse comes to church. My friend, the devil attends church. Others say to me that I can get him saved once we are married. Why not get him saved before you are married? The truth is you can't get him, or anyone saved. It is the work of the Holy Spirit. Do not rush into a marriage period! We marry for all the wrong reasons. Then, we want God to bail us out. Let your future spouse show some Christian fruit before you get married. I cannot tell you the number of times I hear, if only I have waited. Then, it's too late. You made the choice and sadly there are consequences for bad choices. Why go through the struggle when you can say let's wait and receive counseling first?

Review Questions:

1. What projects have you worked together as a team?

2. Have your experience abuse from your partner? What was the result?

3. What do each of you bring to the marriage table?

4. Have both of you made a commitment to follow Jesus Christ. If not, make a commitment to Him right now by asking Him to come into your life and help you in your marriage and in your family.

5. Do you go to the same church? Why or why not?

Chapter Five

DECIDE TO BE A SUBMITTED PARTNER

Submit to One Another out of reverence for Christ.
Ephesians 5:21 NIV

The late Miles Monroe stated in a sermon that when one does not know the purpose of a thing or someone, then abuse occurs. If one does not know the purpose of children, you have child abuse. If one does not know the purpose of drugs, you have drug abuse. Likewise, when one does not know the purpose of marriage, you have marriage abuse or marriage disfunction. How does one learn to be a wife, husband, mother, or a father? It takes years of schooling to become a nurse or doctor. It takes many months of training to become a fireman or a police officer. Yet, there is little education or training to become a spouse or a parent, not to mention mixed marriages. Is it any wonder that many marriages break down? They have not received the necessary education or training to get their marriage off to a good start or a strong foundation. I hear men say

that I don't need counseling. I don't want anyone in our business. Yet, the banks are in their business. The car dealership is in their business. The mortgage company is in their business. Yet, when it come to having a successful and wonderful marriage, we don't want counselors in our business. Yet, when the marriage is collapsing, when the fire of passion is gone, when the kids are separated from a parent, now they want counseling. Why! It like building a house without blueprints and wonder why the house is not what they expected. There were not guidance or blueprint in building the house they wanted. Sadly, there is little guidance in building the marriage they wanted. Unless the Lord builds the house, they labor in vain. Psalms 127:1. God has the blueprint for a long and successful marriage. The Lord knows the challenges and struggles that couples will have in their marriage. It could be financial issues, health issues, infidelity issues, or loneliness issues to name a few. You may say loneliness? I am married. Many married people become lonely when their spouse has checked out of their marriage through work, hobbies, and other activities. Yes, one can become lonely even in their marriage. Now, the hard question. What tools do you have to rebuild your marriage? What tools did you develop to improve your marriage, so every day would be like heaven on earth? I never said that you would not have challenges. Life is full of challenges! Like the house that the wind tries to tear down, it doesn't budge, because it is built on a solid foundation. Our foundation is the Word of God! May, I ask you, "What is the foundation that your marriage is build on?" The foundation could be pleasure, sex, fun, excitement, and many other external things. The truth is that pleasure, sex, and excitement are not always constant. Financial difficulty and responsibility cut right into that pleasure time. Then what do you have left but a shell of a marriage. No substance at all. The fun was great, but no substance. The sex was exciting, but no substance. Every marriage needs specific tools to help them in challenging times like when arguments develop. Are you so in love that you think there will not be any arguments or disagreements? If so, I have a house to sell you. It's a slum house but through your love for one another, you won't notice how bad it is. Your love has blinded you to reality.

Preparation for marriage requires counseling. What company would hire you and not give you training? One is destined to fail because no training for the tasks were given. Likewise, one should receive training before and after marriage. Again, married people need tools to develop and sustain their marriage through tough times. Let me ask you a question. If millions of people are so in love, why did their marriage end in divorce? Couldn't their love for each other sustain them during tough times? Celebrities get divorce. Millionaires get divorce. Couldn't their money sustain them during challenging times. Pastors and ministers get divorce. What's the common denominator in divorce? It can't be money since many are financially wealthy. Could it be that they did not build or develop their marriage on a solid foundation? Counseling cannot save one's marriage. The counselor can only give a couple tools to follow, but each couple must be willing to apply the tools where needed. In building a house, you will need a saw. Other times you may need a hammer or a screwdriver. Whatever the problem, one must pick up the tool and apply it to where it is needed. One may need to pick up the tool of forgiveness. One may need to pick up the tool of patience or the tool of peace. How can you pick up these tools if you do not have them or develop them during the good times in your marriage?

Review Questions:

1. What is the importance of submitting to one another?

2. Why do some couples refuse marriage sessions?

3. What tools are needed in your marriage?

4. How educated are you in becoming a husband or a wife?

5. What is the foundation of your marriage? And why?

Chapter Six

MARRIAGE MAINTENANCE

*Let each one of you love his wife as himself, and let
the wife see that she respects her husband.*
Ephesians 5:33 ESV

One winter morning, I was on my way to work. I needed to be there on time to complete a project. However, my car overheated, and I did not make it to work that day. After I was towed to the nearest service station, I was told that I needed a new water hose. It was worn out with a hole in it. Smoke was everywhere. This could have been avoided if I had regular checkups on my car. Because I ignored having regular checkups on my car, it broke down. Do you know that without regular maintenance on your marriage, it can break down too? Some understand the importance of regular maintenance on their cars by getting the oil change every three months, checking the fluids, and the tires. However, when it comes to one's marriage, there is little or no maintenance until the marriage breaks down. The degree of neglect will determine if the marriage can be saved. Some mechanics will tell you since your car has been neglected for years, it is impossible to fix. It is time to get a new car. My friend, *that is the problem. We neglect our spouse for many years until one says, "we are incompatible, and I need a new spouse." Even if you get a new car or a new spouse and continue to neglect the maintenance on both, you will still have the same problems and sadly, the same results!*

Let's do something different! Let's begin to have honest conversations about what is going on inside of us and in our marriage. One spouse may communicate that I feel neglected and lonely. The other spouse yells, "What do you want me to do! Quit my job!" Do you see the problem right there? The husband and wife are communicating how they feel. The spouse was not asked to quit their job, and your spouse did not ask to be yelled at. One would not yell at the tire that is going flat at an inopportune time, or would you? Remember, you are one! You are a team. Therefore, be willing to listen without being defensive and seek to help your spouse from feeling neglected and lonely. Did you spend many hours on your own hobbies? When was the last time there was real, heartfelt conversation? When was the last time you had fun together doing something that you both enjoyed? Is your ministry at church, taking your time away from your spouse, and all she receives is the leftovers of your time? One must evaluate why the love of your life is feeling so neglected and lonely. Other things may be consuming your time and not your spouse. You may need a new starter! Start over and trace your steps as to when you began to neglect your spouse. Was it that new job or promotion? Did it begin with that new hobby that left your spouse out? Regular maintenance will help you avoid major problems. However, neglect of regular maintenance will turn a minor problem into a major problem, and sometimes it is too late to fix! Do not let them happen to you.

Just as a car can overheat, so can a marriage without the necessary maintenance. Yes, we can disagree, but not to the point that smoke is coming from our ears, eyes, and mouth. Where is the love? Do I love my spouse so much that I am willing to take the time and have maintenance done on our marriage? We take the time to have maintenance on our cars, appliances, and things that we need. Well, don't we need our spouse, or is it easier to just get another spouse? Remember, the grass always appears greener on the other side. However, the other side of the grass is dirt, and worms. It would have been better just to work things out with your spouse than giving up on your marriage. Your new spouse will have issues too! Besides, you are not perfect either! Why blame others and not yourself?

Communication is like oil to the car. Without oil in the car, the car will die. Without honest communication, the marriage will die. It is imperative to keep oil in your marriage. Talk about things that concerns you. Talk about past hurts so you can have closure. Remember, past hurts and past scars just doesn't go away. It can affect your present and future situation. Communication speaks of talking and listening. The problem is we are so busy that we don't have time to listen and that is sad! Listening requires a commitment to focus on what your spouse is saying but also seeking to understand how your spouse feels. We show people that we love them when we are willing to take the time to listen. We cannot say we love our spouse and refuse to listen. We are sending the wrong message. What they are saying, and feeling are not important to me. I remember the time I came home from work, and I was tired, hungry, and sleepy. That is a bad combination. I sat down at the kitchen table, and my wife began to share her heart. It was 5:00 P.M. She shared about her family, and how she wanted her entire family to come and know the Lord. When I looked up at the clock in the kitchen, it was 5:15P.M., and I never said a word. She continued to talk as she prepared dinner. She began to wipe the tears from her eyes as she spoke. The next time I looked at the clock it was 5:30 P.M. In my mind, I was thinking that Rochelle talked non-stop for half an hour, and I did not say a word. I did not give her any of my wisdom, nor did I give her Bible scriptures. I just listened! What I gave her was what she needed. She needed a listening ear. I was surprised that after the half hour of listening she said, "Thank-you for listening; I feel so much better!" I didn't say anything, but I did what she needed! I listened! My friends, I'm telling you with all my heart, take the time to listen to your spouse, to your children, and even to your parents. Listen with your heart and not just your ears. Don't you think they have your best interest at heart?

If not, there may be more than surface issues, and you may need to talk your pastor, church leader, or even a professional counselor.

Patience is like anti-free to your car. Anti-free keeps the car from overheating. The Bible says that love is Patient. I Corinthians 13:4. Love does not go off the handle when your spouse makes a mistake. We must consider the fact that we have made mistakes also. Patience is willing to accept the shortcomings of one's spouse without getting angry or screaming. You burned the dinner! That is not the fruit of patience. Do you have any shortcomings? If you say no, you have at least one that I know. You are a liar! We all have shortcomings. We all can grow! No one is perfect not even you! Give your spouse space to grow. After all, you married him or her even with their faults. Why not work on shortcomings together?

Anti-freeze in the car keeps it from overheating. If you would allow the Word of God and the Holy Spirit to work on your anger issues, your marriage will be so much better. When the car overheats, it's usually not at a good time or place. You could be on the expressway stuck in traffic, and you began to smell smoke. You look all around to see whose car is smoking, and it's yours! You are stuck in traffic and holding up the traffic. Cars are honking at you to move over but the car is not moving. What can you do? You wonder why they are so impatient with you? Don't they understand that your car broke down? Your spouse is broken down through the lack of caring and affection, through unemployment, sickness, or overwhelmed with chores. Your spouse may be broken down through a lack of communication and loneliness, but you are constantly honking at your spouse. That is not the solution. In your overheated car, someone gets out their car to help push you to the side and asks, "What else can I do for you?" Instead of honking at your spouse, why not ask, "What can I do to assist you more?" Now, you are talking! Now, you are sharing yourself to find a solution to the situation. That is patience.

God has been patient with mankind. Through years and years of rebellion and disobedient, He never gave up on us. Can you see the patience of God? His love for you and I caused Him to demonstrate patience to us. The Bible says that while we were sinners Christ died for us. Romans 5:8. God gave His only begotten Son to die on the cross for something He did not do. He took our sins upon Himself and died the death of a criminal because He loved us so! The next time you are ready to explode on your spouse. Remember the cross! Don't forget the cross!

Windshield wipers *help you to see the road more clearly. When you fail to add wiper fluid, you are at a disadvantage since our vision will be cloudy. Married couples must have clear vision to see the dangerous road. Clear vision will help you avoid the unexpected potholes or the out-of-control car who ran the stop sign. Without clear vision, your vehicle can be destroyed in a collision. Marriages are destroyed because they lost their vision. They lost the vision to cherish, care, and respect one another. The Bible says that where there is no vision the people perish. Proverbs 29:18. Your marriage will fail without vision. Vision is seeing what is down the horizon and prepare for what is coming. When a new addition is coming to the home, you have nine months to prepare for that bundle of joy, a gift from God. One does not wait until the baby comes to buy baby clothes, bassinet, or baby supplies. You see down the road that our baby is coming, so you make preparation. The same way one makes preparation for a baby; you must make preparation for a successful marriage.*

Clear vision starts by making Jesus Christ a priority in your marriage. Together, you seek His face for direction in your marriage. You must put everything on the table, your dreams, your goals, and your desires. What do you want from your marriage? What do you want from your spouse? What do your spouse want from you? How can your marriage bring glory to God? How can our marriage remain strong during difficult times? These are serious questions that need answers. Having clear vision will help you see danger signs in your marriage. Don't allow small danger signs to become huge marriage problems. Get them while they are small.

Clear vision will help you make wise decisions. You may not be able to afford that new car right now since you are buying a house. Clear vision says, Let's get our credit score up before we start looking for a house. Couples must learn to stay within their budget. I have seen to many celebrities, rich folks, and poor folks lose their money and family due to a lack of clear vision. Millionaires and professional athletes can't pay their child support for their children. They were under the impression that the gravy train would never run out. Movie stars and athletes cannot get work. Battered fighters must come out of retirement to get another paycheck which will go to good, old Uncle Sam. This happens repeatedly, and only a few have learned from the mistakes of others. Wise up now! See what is down the road. This pandemic caught the world by surprise. People could not pay their rent. Others could not keep up their mortgage payments. Many jobs closed, and people were living from paycheck to paycheck. Who would have thought that people from all races and backgrounds would be in food lines to feed their family? Let's began to have clear vision today!

Discussion Questions:

1. Why should we not neglect our spouse?

2. What is the goal in marriage maintenance?

3. Why is honest communication important in a marriage?

4. What are two ingredients in communication?

5. Explain clear vision in a marriage.

Chapter Seven

THE HUSBAND ROLE TO HIS WIFE

*Husbands, love your wives, even as Christ also
loved the Church, and gave Himself for it.*
Ephesians 5:25.

The husband duty to his wife is more than a duty. It is a role of unselfish love. The husband goes to work out of duty. He goes in the rain, the snow, and even when he is sick. He goes to work faithfully even if he does not like his job. He goes out of duty to be rewarded with a paycheck at the end of the week. If there is no paycheck, there would be no duty. The husband duty is to love his wife. The Apostle Paul tells the Christians in Ephesus to love your wife as Christ loved the church. In a small section in Ephesians Chapter five, the Apostle Paul repeats this statement two more times. As an English teacher, I taught by repetition. Whatever was important, I continued to repeat it as a broken record. If the husband duty to his wife is like his job that he does not like, the marriage is in *trouble from the beginning. Unconditional love says I love you and care to please and serve you. This is more than a duty. When a husband serves out of duty, what happens when there is a major disagreement? What happens when he feels disrespected or ignored? Since he is not being rewarded with a check of respect or a check of attention, the husband is inclined to say this marriage is over!*

What happened? When the husband only serves his wife out of duty like a job, the marriage will collapse. When a man is not happy at his job, he seeks another job. When a man is not happy in his marriage, he seeks another mate. Instead of finding the root cause in his marriage, he looks for someone else not realizing that he is part of the problem. Even if he gets married again, the same problems will occur. Oh! It may be great for a while but when he stops being rewarded for his duties, it's time to move on. This cycle can be repeated many, many times. Why not break the cycle of separation and divorce by doing something different? Begin by examining your own life. Ask yourself the tough questions! Do I love my wife unconditionally? That is, there is nothing that she does that would prevent me from showing love to her. The Apostle Paul says husbands love your wives as Christ loved the church. Ephesians 5:25. Christ demonstrated His love for us not out of duty but love. Christ provided for His church. Christ protected His church. Christ comforted His church. Christ equipped His church. Christ saved His church. Christ prayed for His church. Christ died for His church. Does this sound like something someone would do out of duty when the recipients were rebellious, disrespectful, and disobedient? Despite that, His love was constant!

The husband role is to love his wife unconditionally. It is serving with love. The husband role is to provide care for his wife. The husband must anticipate what she needs and provide it. The husband role is to protect her from harm. The husband must protect her from scams and wicked people. The husband role is to take the stress off his wife. Our wives were not built to manage stress even though many do. The husband role is to have open and honest conversation with her. Let her into your world. Share your weaknesses and problems with her.

She will appreciate that more than you know. The husband role is to provide affection, not sex, but affection to his wife. This affection speaks of holding, touching, hugging, and expressing love and appreciation towards the woman that you married. Husbands, let us not take our wives for granted. This year will mark our 40th anniversary, and I still see the gleam in her eyes for her husband. I am so happy about that. It's a joy for me to serve my wife. Yes, it is part of my role. I refuse to be a public success at church and a private failure at home. We enjoy each other company. It does not matter if we are on a cruise or watching a movie at home, we are happy together. Let's serve our wives not out of duty but with a love that will last forever!

Discussion Questions:

1. What is unselfish love?

2. How can a husband anticipate what his wife needs?

3. Is it hard for you to share your heart with your wife? Why?

4. How do you show your wife that you love her?

5. What ways this week have you expressed love to her? If not, do it today!

Chapter Eight

THE WIFE ROLE TO HER HUSBAND

> **Wives, submit yourselves unto your own husband, as unto the Lord.**
> *Ephesians 5:22*

The role of the wife is more than a duty. It is a duty of love and sacrifice. This duty is expressed by her submissiveness to her husband, not a doormat nor a wife without a voice. There can be no teamwork in a marriage when the wife has no voice. She must be able to speak honestly about what is on her mind. I know that many women today frown on the thought of being a submissive wife. Either God knows what He is doing, or He doesn't. Either He knows what is best for the family or He doesn't. Either we trust the Lord, or we don't. God created our world and created the family. He wants the family to be successful, prosperous, and blessed, so He gave guidelines for us to follow to ensure that our family will be strong. Decide to obey the Lord! The problem comes when the husband or the wife refuse to follow God's directions for a successful home. Many wives have not idea of the influence she has on her husband. As a young newlywed, I was trying to find my way and serve the Lord with all my heart. I was not making a lot of money and was in tremendous debt. I was asked by my church leaders to become a deacon. They did not know the debt I was in! They only knew me from church. However, my wife knew all my weaknesses. We lived in an apartment at the time. Several times, the gas and electric company would come and shut us down. You cannot imagine how hurt and embarrassed I was. How could I ask my wife if she thought I could be a good deacon or leader in the church? We had no lights! I waited since I knew she would tell me the truth. Finally, I asked her, "Rochelle, do you think I have leadership qualities." She did not hesitate and said, "Yes." I was so happy! Here's the point. If she would have said no, I would not have accepted the position of deacon at my church. If my wife doesn't see me as a leader, why should others? I would not be an assistant pastor or an elder today. I served ten years as a deacon and trained other leaders from more than twenty-five churches. Your role is to believe the best in your husband. My wife believed in me, and it had a tremendous impact on our lives. Let me caution you. Your submissiveness to your husband does not mean accepting mental and physical abuse. You have the God-given right to protect yourself and your children from abuse. I know this is in conflict to some teaching today. However, God has called us to peace. There is no peace in the home where there is mental and physical abuse. The best way to help your spouse and children is to get a restraining order and to find a safe place to live. You can encourage him from a distance to get help. Through prayer and counseling, you may discover where his abuse originated from.

We have been out of debt for many years now. We assisted in helping our children get through college without too much debt. I worked a part-time job to assist in this area. In the early years, my credit score was 630. Well, I am at 835! The Lord has helped me along with an encouraging wife. She never screamed at me when the gas or electric was cut off. That always stood out to me. Ladies, you have the power to influence *your husband in a positive way! Be a praying woman, relying on God for wisdom and direction.*

Allow your husband to lead. I had counseling sessions where the wife complained that her husband refused to lead. A husband shared that he had five sisters older than him, so he never had to lead. As we studied his role as a husband, slowly he began to lead his family. This humble man has grown into a leader at home and a leader in the church. However, some wives refuse to let the husband lead after they complain that they want their husband to lead. Wives, husbands cannot lead if you refuse to follow. If your church is having three nights of revival, and your husband requests you accompany him on a trip and you refuse to follow him. What message are you sending? If your husband gives you a limit on your credit card, and you go over it by $500.00, what message are you sending? You're saying, "I don't have to listen to you since this is my credit card."

Another session involved a couple whose wife wanted to purchase some expensive jewelry. She asked her husband, but he said not at this time. He wanted to get the bills under control. The next day she came home with the new and expensive jewelry. Why ask your husband if you are going to do what you want anyway? She may have made more money than her husband. However, that is no excuse for not being a submissive wife. It is God who gave us principles to follow. When we disobey His principles, there will be consequences for our disobedience. He knows what He is doing. When we follow His principles, The Lord can make a great change in you and in your husband as well.

Discussion Questions:

1. Why is it hard for some wives to be submissive to their husband?

2. Explain the difference between a submissive wife and a wife with no voice.

3. What goals are you working on together?

4. Do you have the freedom to share your heart to your husband?

5. Do you have to be a submissive wife if your husband is mentality or physically abusing you? If yes, what should you do?

Standing:
Marcus Bishop, Andrea Bishop, Maurice and
Jekerra Bishop, Amari Flowers

Sitting:
Norman and Rochelle Bishop

Chapter Nine
A DEAL BREAKER

> **Follow thou not an unjust man (Do not follow a**
> **lawbreaker) Follow thou not his ways.**
> *Proverbs 3:31 WYC*

If you are engaged to be married, is there a deal breaker in your engagement? Is there something in your relationship or present situation that would cause you to call off your engagement? For example, if your future spouse hits you, would that be a deal breaker? If your fiancé hits you and break your nose, would that be a deal breaker? If your fiancé puts a gun up to your head, would that be a deal breaker? It has been my experience in many cases, there were very few deal breakers. I could go on with many, more examples. However, I believe you get the point. Are you so in love, you must marry your future spouse regardless of what they do? What about the abuse of your child by the man or woman that you plan to marry? Although your future spouse says they will never do that again, is that a deal breaker for you? Do you have a deal breaker, or is everything acceptable? Are drugs acceptable? Is cheating acceptable? Is not working or not looking to work acceptable to you? You have your man, but he has no job to support the family. Is that acceptable to you? In my many years of counseling sessions, only a few had a deal breaker. Some believed it was an isolated incident. Others believed that they could pray it away. Most believed that after they are married the situation will change. They are right! The situation will change. It will become worse! Marriage does not change who you are. Many people believe they are the exception because they are rich, a celebrity, or a leader in the church. Please understand if one is an abuser before marriage, it is more likely they will be an abuser after marriage. Marriage does not change who you are, and neither will money. If I am selfish before marriage, I will be selfish after marriage. If I am stingy before marriage, I will be stingy after marriage even if I inherit a million dollars. Remember, marriage nor money can change the person only God can do that, and it does not happen overnight! Be prepare to experience some pain if you ignored danger signs, and nothing was a deal breaker for you.

I had a deal breaker, and I did not know it at first. I became friends with Rochelle. She was beautiful on the inside and beautiful on the outside. It was amazing to me that she would go out with me! I was shocked! In my mind, I wondered, "What is wrong with her that she would go out with me?" We dated for five weeks. I was on cloud nine! As we went for a walk, she gave me the bombshell! I knew it was too good to be true. She told me that she had a boyfriend. My balloon burst! Five weeks of dating and going to the movies, to dinner and just enjoying each other company and now this bombshell. I asked her why did you wait all this time to tell me? My last serious relationship I got hurt badly, and it was happening again. She explained that she and her boyfriend decided to take a break due to heated arguments. She decided to tell him that she was dating me and that it was over between them. I was elated to hear that! After just five weeks of dating, I wanted to spend my life with her!

When I arrived at church the next Sunday, I saw her in the lobby. As I was walking towards her, her boyfriend or ex boyfriend greeted her. They greeted each other with a kiss, not on the cheek but in the lips. Those who know me, know how calm I am even under pressure. Well, I went ballistic! Since we were at church, I took her to the side and blasted her for kissing him. That was a deal breaker for me! I told her that you cannot kiss him and kiss me too! If your affection for him is so strong that you need to kiss him then just stay with him. I was done and was prepared to move on. She could have said you will not control who I can or cannot kiss after five weeks of dating. I can kiss whoever I want. There is no ring on my finger. She did not say anything like that. She said okay and apologized. She never kissed him again. Two months later, she asked me, "When were we getting married?" I could not believe that she wanted to marry me. My heart was doing jumping jacks! I was so happy! I looked on the calendar and wrote November fourteenth. It was eleven months away. I never propose to her. That's how insecure I was. This November will be our 40th anniversary. We were married in 1981. Her smile even today still melts my heart! After raising three children, we are still enjoying each other. Now that we are both retired; we can go as we please. I honestly believe that marriage can be heaven on earth when you put Christ first and make it a priority to please each other.

Question again, do you have a deal breaker, or will you accept anything? You may say, "I have my man or my woman." Do you really have your spouse or do someone or something else have your spouse too! Do sex sites have your spouse? Do job and hobbies have your spouse that there is no time for you? Do drugs and alcohol have your spouse? Does your spouse spend all their money gambling that the mortgage is three months behind? Is anything a deal breaker for you? Sad to say, there were very few deal breakers in my sessions. When I pointed out the danger signs, I can only remember two couples that decided to wait. Eventually, they broke up. One female refused to call off the wedding after being physically abused. I would not marry them, so they went some place else. They got married but divorce in less than a year. People who love you and care about your well-being may insist that you don't marry her or him, would you listen? Let me be clear with this statement. We must listen to those who love us. This year I suffered a heart attack and did not know it. I had no appetite, and I only had a little pain. When I drank water, I would throw it up. That gave me a concern.

However, I thought it was just food poisoning. My wife and daughter wanted me to go to emergency, but I did not listen. My dad told them to take me to emergency. They told him I didn't want to go. He stated it is not about what Norman wants but what is needed to get done. As I sat on the sofa, I had this thought. My wife, my daughter, and my dad were not trying to hurt me. I know they love me dearly! It was then another thought came to my mind. Listen to those who love you. Listen to those who love you. I got up, and my daughter and her friend drove me to the emergency department. The doctor told me that my heart was functioning at ten percent. The normal heart functions at fifty percent. I did not know that. The surgeons could not do a bypass because my heart was too weak. After two weeks in the hospital, my surgical team concluded that my heart improved to the point that I did not need a bypass only one stint then maybe two small stints in a couple of months. My surgical team went from my wrist to my heart and completed the surgery in twenty minutes. I had no pain going in, and no pain after the surgery. By the grace of God, they said no other stints were needed. I pray you will remember that statement. Listen to those who love you. At least, consider what they are telling you. Your family and your true friends have your best interest at heart.

Why would anyone want to get married and be miserable for years? That is not God's plan. We must trust Him and wait for His guidance and direction. Sometimes, we can rush into things that are bad decisions with bad consequences. It is my heart desire that you would become so close to the Lord that you will not be pressured or rushed into a marriage that is not God's best for you.

Discussion Questions:

1. If your fiancé is not a Christian, is that a deal breaker for you?

2. Can money save a marriage?

3. In making important decisions in one's life, who should you listen too?

4. What are some deal breakers you might consider?

5. List three reasons why you want to marry your fiancé?

Chapter Ten

THE NEEDS OF THE WIFE

> **Let the husband render to his wife the affection due**
> **her, and likewise, also the wife to her husband.**
> *1 Corinthians 7:3 NKJV*

In the beginning of our marriage, I just wanted to make my wife happy. I wanted to please her, but I was limited in my knowledge of what she needed. I was taught that a wife needs protection, affection, and comfort. However, how was I going to put that into practice on a regular basis? I could not go on my feelings. If we had an argument that day, I may not feel like being affectionate. I am upset with her, so I am withholding affection, protection, and comfort from her. As a husband, you cannot choose when to hold affection, protection, and comfort based on how we feel. If you get fired from your job, your wife still needs affection, protection, and comfort from you. She is your wife and deserve your constant affection. It must be ongoing and not a one-time event or when you feel like it. The needs of your wife should be met by you for a lifetime! Don't be afraid of the word lifetime. Just enjoy the journey even with all the challenges that marriage brings. Marriage can

bring enjoyment and fulfilment. I am telling you what I know! Enjoy the journey with your best friend! You will look back on the journey and say, "Thank-you Jesus for helping us in our challenging times." Let's take a closer look at what a wife needs.

A wife needs **affection,** not just sex. This affection is a strong expression of fondness, caring, and commitment. In my counseling sessions, I would ask the wife; do your husband loves you?" I am saddened when the wife responds with a no, or I am not sure. The husband would try to defend his actions by saying I pay all the bills. Well, paying the bills is what you are doing for her, but affection is what you are doing to her. When was the last time, you took your wife to a romantic place for dinner or purchase flowers for her and not on Valentine Day? Mail her a card saying how much you love her! She will be so surprised, so watch out that night! We marry the woman of our dreams and forget what it takes to keep her. We lose our fire or passion since we have her now. Allow your love to grow. Keep surprising her by doing unexpected things that show how much you love your wife. Listen to me clearly. As you pour on affection, she will pour on affection with respect. I dare you to try it! See what happens! It has been forty years, and I still hold my wife hand and open the car door for her. She is my wife, a gift from God to me and deserve all my affection. Rochelle is the mother of our three, grown-up children. She sacrificed so much for our children, and she put her career on hold to take care of our family. I honor her by my display of affection.

A wife needs **conversation**. I remember clearly when I would come home from work, and my lovely wife would greet me at the door. She would asked, "How was my day?" I would say, "Okay." Rochelle firmly said to me that I am here with your children and need adult conversation. That stood out to me, and I never forgot it. From that point, I had to be intentional about having conversations with my best friend. I had to learn to go in details about what was going on at work, at church, and in our community. It was not easy, but it was what my wife needed. Husbands and husbands to be, take the time to have detailed conversation with your spouse even if you feel a little *uncomfortable. Remember, you want to please your wife. My friend, when you seek to please your wife, you are making positive deposits into her life. Keep depositing good and positive things into her life. You will get a great return! When your money is low, you go to the bank to make a withdraw. It's the same in a marriage. You deposit regularly into your wife. In the course of being married, there will be some disagreements and some intense arguments. You lost your temper! Now is the time to make a withdraw from what you deposited. You deposited love, kindness, patience, and conversation in her. When you take the high road and apologize to her, what you deposited in her will come out. Your wife incubates what you put inside of her. Therefore, if your deposit selfishness and meanness, don't be surprised if you get the same thing back. The Bible tells us that whatever you sow; you will reap. Galatians 6:7. Be wise and deposit the fruit of the Spirit in your wife by your actions. Trust me, you will receive a great return!*

*A wife needs **openness and honesty.** I remember early in our marriage Rochelle wanted openness and honesty. "Just tell me the truth, she would say." Openness and honesty helped her better to deal with present situations. Don't hide the truth! It is imperative to give accurate information. The Bible tells us to speak the truth in love. Ephesians 4:15. It did not say to exaggerate the truth or lie about the truth. Husbands, your wife should be your best friend, so tell her the truth. If she is not your best friend, you must begin to bridge that gap by open and honest communication. Open your heart to her and listen to her heart. Begin to put into practice meeting the needs of your wife. She will notice your efforts and appreciate them.*

*A wife needs **comfort.** One of your responsibilities is to take the stress off your wife. Women were not made to manage so much stress. Women bear our children. Raise our children while working a job. Women take them to school, to the doctors, to the dentists, to school functions, and so much more. She comes home and cook, clean the house, help the children with their homework, give the children a bath, while the husband is watching football, boxing, hockey, basketball, or baseball. Now, it's about 12 midnight, and the husband wants to play. The wife* is exhausted from the day, and it may be worse tomorrow. Now the husband is upset since his wife is supposed to meet his needs. We cannot use Bible verses to get what we want from our wife when we neglected them all day. That is not caring nor being sensitive to the needs of your wife. Why not assist the wife in giving the kids a bath or washing the dishes? The husband may say that I pay the mortgage or rent. There is more to a marriage than just paying bills. Is their peace and comfort in the home? Is your wife happy or miserable? Is there security and comfort in the home? Does the wife have to wonder if the mortgage will be paid this month, or must she find a new place to live? A wife needs stability in the home.

A wife needs **spiritual leadership and family commitment**. I often here in many sessions, "I'm the leader in my home, Pastor Norman." Since you are the leader, why not lead your family in prayer and Bible reading.? Since you are the leader, are you an example of a Christian, inside the church and outside the church? Do your wife and children know with certainty they are a priority to you? Do you spend more time with friends, hobbies and working more than with your family? God knows that a man must work but that is no excuse for neglecting your family. Do you take the family on regular vacations or regular small trips? When our money was tight, we would walk around Penn's Landing and watch the free events. I would buy our three children ice cream. They were happy! Now that they are gown up and out the house, I can look back and thank the Lord for helping me to be the best husband and father I could be. Each year I continue to ask the Lord to make me the best husband and father that I can be to my family along with being a better son to my parents. Husbands, pray and ask the Lord to help you. He wants to help you! He made the family. He wanted a family that would glorify Him. It doesn't mean you will not have problems or challenges. May I tell you; we had many! However, through it all, we learned to trust in Jesus, and He is still helping us today.

Review Questions:

1. What ways can you demonstrate love to your wife?

2. How can you improve your communication skills with your wife?

3. Have you been intentional about bringing comfort to the home?

4. Why is it sometimes hard to speak the truth?

5. What does family commitment means to you?

Chapter Eleven

THE NEEDS OF THE HUSBAND

Let each one of you love his wife as himself, and let
the wife see that she respects her husband.
Ephesians 5:33 ESV

Many years ago, my wife and I were invited to the home of a prominent pastor for dinner. What a huge and beautiful house they had! There is a difference having a beautiful house and a beautiful home. It was equally beautiful on the inside. However, what I remembered the most was how his wife spoke loudly and harshly to her husband. It was not just one time. It was throughout our time with them. My wife and I felt uncomfortable in their presence. The pastor appeared embarrassed and saddened by his wife tone and actions. We don't know what goes on behind closed doors. This was too much for us, and we never went back to visit them again. When we got into our car, I told my wife that whatever I do, please do not disrespect me like that. We agreed it was horrible, and she plead that she would never disrespect me like that, and she has kept that plead. To God be the glory!

A husband needs **respect**. He may not receive respect on his job or even from the people in his community. However, the one place he should receive respect is from his wife and children. Respect speaks of admiration or holding someone in high regard. Now, it would be hard for a wife to hold her husband in high regard if he is an abusive husband, a womanizer, and not responsible in taking care of his family. That situation is not what I am talking about. A family like that would need a lot of work and be willing to listen and accept criticism and advice. Some men and women in our sessions could not accept criticism or advice. I could not help them. I am talking about a husband who is taking care of his family the best he can. Even if the family never say thank you, the husband continues to serve his family. He works every day to provide food, shelter, protection, and care for his family. In that context, he should have earned his wife respect. If the wife does not respect or esteem her husband, there are other women who will. Don't let another woman admire your husband more than you! My wife is my biggest fan. When I graduated from Liberty University with my master's degree in Pastoral Counseling. My wife and daughter missed the bus and had to walk to the stadium. My wife was having trouble with her knee, but she was determined to see me graduate. I would have been fine if she didn't make it because of her knee. It is not easy being responsible for making sure the family has the things that they need. You know if you have a good man or not. If you do, you should appreciate him and not constantly criticize him for his actions. That constant criticism will have a negative affect on him and on your marriage. Your husband needs respect from his wife. Respect says to the wife that I will honor my husband even if I don't agree with his decision. Can you give your husband the benefit that he is trying to take care of the family? Husbands are learning on the job! My wife would tell me that the sink is leaking. I would get my tools and try to fix it. Sometimes I could, and other times I had to call a plumber. Things that I was able to fix she would be so proud of me saving money for the family! I can tell you that made me so happy. She was proud of her man! Wives would do well by showing respect and admiration to their own husband. Why would wives show more esteem and admiration to another man that is not taking care of them or her children?

A husband needs **sexual fulfillment.** The family and sex were created and ordained by God. Everything He created was good! However, sin has a way of taking good and making it bad. Sin has a way of making right wrong and making clean dirty. The Bible tells us, let thy fountain be blessed, and rejoice with the wife of thy youth. Let her be as the loving hind and pleasant roe; Let her breasts always satisfy thee; And be thou ravished always with her love. Proverbs 5:18-19. That's the Word of God! That is not spiritual but physical. It is important that the wife care for her husband in this way. The wife should ask her husband if she can go on a missionary trip to Africa for two months. Some wives have been bold enough to tell their husband they are going on a missionary trip for a couple of months. One husband said that is fine. When the wife makes decisions without the consent of her husband, she is asking for problems. Where is the teamwork that we talked about earlier? I have seen in our sessions how wives would hold sex from their husband unless he did what she asks. You cannot hold your husband hostage. That is not what the Bible teaches. What if the husband say that I am not paying any bills unless you come with me on vacation? Love is not selfish but looks out for their partner. If one would ask, how would this decision affect my husband? We would not make certain decisions. The wife does not have authority over her own body but yield it to her husband. In the same way, the husband does not have authority over his own body but yield it to his wife.

1 Corinthians 7:4. NIV. This attitude shows unselfishness and the willingness to work together as a team and meeting each other needs.

A husband needs an **attractive spouse.** It does not mean that he needs someone who looks like Hollywood celebrities. No, he needs a wife that will look the best she can and willingly take care of her body. She wants to please her husband by her attractiveness. There is nothing wrong with that! Let me say here. If your husband demands that you get all these artificial treatments to enhance your body, so he will be attractive to you, he should already be attractive to you by *the person you are.. From that point, it's about getting to know one another. People marry on looks without knowing the person they are marrying. We talked about that in chapter two on reasons why people get married. Think about this, you were campus queen in college, simply beautiful and intelligent. You get married to this tall and handsome man. However, five years later, you develop cancer and had to lose both your breasts, or you were in a car accident and lost your right arm. Will your man still love you unconditionally? Will his love for you transcends physical attraction? Yes, physical attraction is important to a husband. However, love for our wives must be stronger that physical attraction. The wife should want to look good for her husband. I remember a woman in our counseling session stated that her husband should accept the way she looks now. He is a church leader, so he will not leave me. Her hair was a mess, her clothes were old fashion, and she was close to three hundred pounds at five feet, five inches. The husband insisted that she go to weight watcher and to Planet Fitness, and he would go with her. She refused. She wanted her husband to love and care for her regardless of her outward appearance. Through our sessions, she began to understand the importance of looking the best she could for her husband. It took extra sessions, but I was so happy that she finally adjusted her lifestyle to enhance her beauty. Ladies, if your husband is a womanizer, you can make all the adjustments you want, and he still will not be happy with you. Therefore, make sure you love yourself first! You cannot control what your husband will do.*

*A husband needs **domestic assistance**. There are some men who just do not know how to iron, cook, wash clothes, change diapers, and the list goes on. Some husbands can't pick out the right furniture that will go with the right room. I couldn't. Even now, I tell my wife to pick the furniture she wants, and I will pay the bill. Truthfully, I could care less about the color coordination in our home if Rochelle is happy, then I am happy. I am embarrassed to tell you how long we had our bedroom furniture. She bought it before we were married. It didn't even bother me that it was falling apart. It bothered her, so we purchased a brand, new bedroom set. Guess who picked out everything. She did! It* is a blessing to make my wife happy. She doesn't ask for much but give me so much joy!

I learned how to cook, iron, and wash clothes at an early age. I taught my boys to do the same at an early age. I did not want them to depend on someone to cook all their food, and iron all their clothes. When they marry, they will be able to assist in taking care of the house if the wife is sick or away. I do most of the cooking in our home for years. I iron my own clothes, and we take turns washing each other clothes. What a joy I have in serving my family! I often say that I cannot serve in the church if I cannot serve at home. My service at church starts from my service at home. My love for my church family starts from my love at home with my wife, children, and my parents.

A husband needs a **fun and hobby companion.** When I was dating my wife, I played in a Christian basketball league. Players would bring their wives, kids, and friends to the game. We kept stats on scoring, rebounds, assist, and steals. It was a joy to have my wife support, cheering for her man to make a basketball. I also played in many, tennis tournaments, and some were for prize money. However, I won trophies but no money. I just loved to play. I was a member of the United States Tennis Association and played number one seed on my team. I loved my basketball team, the basketball league, and my tennis team. I was the only Black person on my tennis team. They really supported me. One day I took my future spouse to the tennis court. She continued to hit the ball over the fence. Tennis was not her sport! I did not care. Tennis was not why I wanted to marry her. Rochelle was beautiful on the inside and beautiful on the outside. She had an unconditional love for me that I could never even imagine. Rochelle loved to bowl and take long walks. We participated in our church bowling league and came in second place. After forty years of marriage, we still have hobbies and enjoy each other company. Hobbies today does not include basketball or tennis. It includes going different places out of the country. It includes going to shows, shopping, Sixer's games or watching the Philadelphia Eagles. We have board games also. I do zoom classes on various topics and conduct our home cell groups through conference calls. My wife is supportive in all I do! I do not take that for granted!

Review Questions:

1. What does a wife gain by respecting her husband?

2. What does a wife lose by disrespecting her husband?

3. What is the purpose of sex?

4. Explain Proverbs 5:18-19 in your own words

5. Why should the wife keep her personal, appearance up?

6. Should spouses share the domestic chores?

7. What hobbies do you share together?

Chapter Twelve

RAISING GODLY CHILDREN

> *Train up a child in the way he should go, and*
> *when he is old, he will not depart from it.*
> Proverbs 22:6 NKJV

It takes time to train our children. Therefore, it is imperative that we spend time with them. Society makes it hard on parents to spend quality time with their children since so much is required of them. Both parents may have to work due to their financial situation. They want to put their children in the best schools and that takes money. There are meetings and training sessions that jobs require. One must attend parent teacher's meeting. One must prepare dinner, pay the bills, make dentist, and doctor appointments for the kids. This does not includes playing board games or sport games with the kids. With all these things, where is the time to train our kids and what are we training them in? The training of our children is the responsibility of the parents. We cannot leave the training to teachers or anyone else. Since we decided to have kids, training is needed for the children and in many cases for the parents also. Where will the parent training come from? Will it come from their parents? If their parents training came from their parents who was never taught how to raise their own children, we will just be making the same mistakes as our parents. What are we to train them in? We should train our children to have a personal relationship with Jesus Christ and impart godly principles and wisdom that will govern their lives. My friend, we can give our children a lot of money and material things. However, if we give them godly principles along with wisdom, our children will have strong character to meet the challenges that they will face in life. The Bible says that even when they are old, these truths will remain with them. As I watch my three, grown up children, I am proud of each one of them. My wife and I began to have family devotions with them from first grade until they graduated from high school. Our devotions lasted about ten minutes each day. Before they went to school, one of us would share scriptures and pray over them. This was normal in our household. When I had to be at work early, then Rochelle would do devotions. As the kids grew, they began to pray and read the Bible and ask questions. As they prepared for college, I wanted to know if what we put in them really worked. I heard too many horror stories about when children left home for college. It was like they had the freedom to do anything they wanted. Some came back home with a different look, tattoos all over their body. Some came back home with a different, worldly attitude and outlook. There was no talk about Jesus or church! Now, our children made their share of mistakes like all of us. The Bible says that all have sinned and fall short of the glory of God. Romans 3:23. However, godly principles will not leave your children even when they become old. What great news! That is what the Bible teaches. It is something that we can give our children that will stay with them for a lifetime. Parents leave money to their children, but it can all be gone. Listen to this, In the blink of an eye wealth disappears, for it sprout winds and fly away like an eagle. Proverbs 23:5 NLT. Many athletes and celebrities have lost million of dollars for many reasons. You know that is the truth. Thank God that many recovered from their lost but not all.

As I mentioned earlier, I am proud of my children. God has blessed our family. We have challenges like any family. It is our commitment to Christ as a family that has made the difference. Today was Father's Day, and I was blessed with many gifts. They have already given me the greatest gift many years ago. It was their commitment to live by the godly principles they were taught as a child and by our example of living a Christian life before them. If one just teaches and train their children without being an example, it shows inconsistencies and confuses them. You tell them not to smoke, and they see you smoking. It confuses them. Your children will remember what you did and didn't do. Our daughter, Andrea, called me at work and asked what I was doing. I told her that I was working and what she needed. Andrea is an adult with her own apartment and car. She remembered how I would take her out for father and daughter night out. She could pick any restaurants she wanted, and we would go there. As a teen-ager, I could not believe that she knew all these expensive restaurants! I made the promise and had to keep it. It made us closer even to this day. She called and wanted to know if we could continue our father and daughter night out. I said, "yes!" She drove to my job, and she took me to one of those expensive restaurants. She loves her dad, and her dad loves her, and she knows it, and my sons know it also! Just as the Lord will always be there for me, I will always be there for my grown-up children.

I understand that couples may have accepted Christ after they were married and had children. They were not brought up in a Christian home or taught godly principles. All is not lost. In one of my leadership classes, one of the church leaders said that he was not a good father to his son before Christ. He neglected his family and there was bad blood between the two. He asked, "What can I do to turn our relationship around?" I thanked him for sharing his heart and being vulnerable during our church leadership class. It is no harm not knowing what to do. It is not asking for help when you need it. I told this humble man to sit down with his son and apologize to him for his behavior. With tears in his eyes, he then asked his adult son to forgive him. His son already saw the change in his dad, but he was not convinced that this change would last. Before our five sessions were over, the man testified *before our class that their relationship had been restored and his son accepted Christ as his Savior. Through his humility, he gained his son back. It wasn't by yelling or by force. It was by living a godly life before his family and willing to humble himself and apologize for the things he neglected to do with his son. My friend, this book is to help you. You may never be in any classes I teach, or ever hear me preach a message, or sit in a counseling session with me, but understand that this book is my class and my message to you. I want your marriage and your family to be strong. I am giving you forty years of my marriage experience along with forty years of advising and counseling newlyweds, married couples, and pre-marriage couples. This is real life to me. That is why I choose to be transparent with you and share my mistakes, so you can avoid the pitfalls that I made by not making wise decisions. That is why I never charge anyone a fee for my services.*

Look at our society. We see the gun violence all around our country. We hear all the debates on what should be done. Let the teachers have guns. Let the church leaders come to church packing. Let's do gun buyback. Let's protest to make our schools and neighborhoods safer. Let's make stiffer gun laws, so young people or bad people can't get guns. Have you heard anyone say, let's start with training our children in godly principles, and let the parents be examples of the godly principles they teach to their children? You will not hear that on a consistent basis! It costs too much! Children are being bullied at school. Children are being abused at home. Children are being murdered on the streets. As a nation, we lost our way. Our money says, "In God we trust," we don't trust Him. We trust in our money, and in our government. If we trust God, why was prayer and Bible reading taken from our school by law? We replaced prayer and Bible reading with guns and drugs in our schools. We asked Congress to do something. What can they do? They are divided on many levels and on polices also. Remember, a house divided cannot stand. Matthew 12:25. Congress cannot change the heart of anyone only Jesus can do that! I hear that God is the blame for the downfall of our nation. Yet, He gave us principles to follow, and we refuse to listen! We wanted freedom to do what we want. Now, we must face the consequences of our decisions. God created and ordained the family. He wanted the family to walk in His principles, so the family would show the glory of God. When there is a breakdown in the family, it affects our churches, our schools, and our nation. No amount of money can restore our nation back to God. It will take repentance and humility to restore our nation back to God. No laws can change the human heart.

I remember saying the pledge of allegiance in school along with praying and Bible reading. Many of our children are void of the knowledge of God today. They don't know that He loves them and want them to be a part of His family. They don't know why He sent His only, begotten Son to the cross. They don't know that God has a plan for their life. Is it any wonder that young adults grow up with no value for human life? They hurt and kill without conscience. We need God in our homes and the willingness to teach our children godly principles and be an example before them. Yesterday, I saw an old video of my sons thanking their mother and I for the godly teaching they received. My youngest son was in college, and my oldest young was in the Army. Each have their own journey, but God's Word will continue to follow them. Our teaching must be a priority. If we do not instruct our children, the streets will teach them and gobble them up. We have a job to do. I live in South Philadelphia and tried to get a place where I could teach children how to read and write and give godly principles. I filled out applications with no response back. I was going to buy all the supplies. I just needed a place to teach the children. I believe people want to do something but are hindered by many reasons and excuses. Our kids suffer.

Raising children from blended families bring a lot of challenges to consider before marriage. Since each family and children are different, open communication in dealing with the present situation and future endeavors are extremely important. There are things to consider before marriage. Do my children like the person I plan on marrying? How old are our children? What is the age gap? There may be some resentment from the children. One may feel you are taking their parent away from them and refuse to respect the new parent. Seek to build a relationship naturally and never treat one child different from the others. Kids notice things and will be silent about it. If one parent brings ice cream for his blood son and nothing for his new son, it will not be forgotten. You cannot punish one for not cleaning her room while the others are not punished for their dirty room. If the kids see you arguing and getting physical, kids will take the side of their blood parent. It will be hard to restore that relationship. I believe the key is open and honest communication and building a strong relationship with the children. They need to know that you are there for the long haul. When problems occur, one party doesn't abandon the family. The children must know that you love and care for them. That takes time! It is more than giving them a gift for their birthday or a present at Christmas. It is each day showing unconditional love for them. I had sessions where things worked out very well, and others were a disaster! I will share one or two counsel sessions on blended families.

Review Questions:

1. Do you see godly training as an investment in your children?

2. What activities prevent parents from training their children? What specific changes can be made immediately?

3. Have you discovered the God given gifts in your children?

4. Have you considered the responsibility of a blended family?

5. What are some challenges you see in a blended family and how do you plan to overcome these obstacles?

Chapter Thirteen

THERE IS HOPE FOR YOU!

Being confident of this, that He who began a good work in you
will carry it on to completion until the day of Christ Jesus.
Philippians 1:6 NIV

You may be separated from your spouse or even divorce. I am saying that there is still hope for you. However, you must be willing to make changes to your life. First, acknowledge what you contributed to the separation or the divorce. Own up to it! In Psalms 51, King David acknowledges his sin and confessed it. He did not blame Bathsheba at all! We must never forget that God is full of mercy towards us. Ephesians 2:4-5. Therefore, we must be full of mercy towards the person we separated from or divorced from. How can we be spiteful when God has shown us mercy for our disobedience and sins? It is extremely important that one does not seek to destroy the character of the spouse or destroy them financially. God said, "Do not avenge yourselves, but rather give place unto wrath, for it is written, Vengeance is mine, and I will repay." Romans 12:19. When a spouse seeks revenge, God will hold His revenge on the other spouse. It is clear in scriptures that Christians must practice love and *forgiveness! One spouse may be entitled to an extremely large settlement by the court. However, it may mean that the mother of the children will lose her home. Why would you allow that to happen? Do you despised your spouse so much that you want the worse for her or him? That is not showing the fruit of the Spirit found in Galatians 5:22. God cannot bless you when you are displaying so much hate and bitterness towards your spouse. Allow God to impart justice to the both of you. Seek to walk in forgiveness. Forgiveness is to pardon whole heartedly and not holding a grudge. Let the man see his children and allow the woman to see her children also. There may need to be some restrictions depending on the situation. That is okay. The point is how can God bless you when you show meanness towards the one you were married to? Finally! Be committed to Christ! Give Him charge over your life! You ran your life for many years, and it ended in discouragement and failure. That can change today! True satisfaction comes from a relationship with Jesus Christ. Decide to follow Christ with all your heart and that will be the best decision you will ever make!*

Contrary to people beliefs, divorce is not the unpardonable sin. Members of churches get divorce. Church leaders get divorce. Pastors and Bishop's get divorce and keep on preaching. I believe this happens when there is no accountability. No one is above accountability. Malachi 2:16 says that God hates divorce. He also hates a proud look and a lying tongue. He hates hands that shed innocence blood. Proverbs 6:16-19. He did not say that one could not be forgiven for having a proud look or forgiveness for lying. Man, where would we be if He did not forgive us for lying, even though He hates it. God lets us know what He loves and what He hates. In other words, He has a standard that is clear! Since He hates a proud look, He loves a humble look or a humble attitude. Since He hates a lying tongue, He loves a mouth that speaks the truth in love. All the things God hates in Proverbs 6:16-19, the opposite is what He loves. God hates hand that shed innocence blood. Therefore, He loves hands that save lives. God hates divorce because it destroys families. It was God who created and wanted a family. He wanted the family to show forth His glory upon the earth. I am sure you know that whatever God loves, the devil hates. Therefore, he wants to destroy the family by any means necessary. Marriage is about a man marrying a woman. Marriage is honorable, and the bed undefiled. Hebrews 13:4. God designed it so that the couple would bring and raise godly children upon the earth. Divorce hinders this work. The answer is clear. Are you going to follow the principles in His Word or follow what you want to do? You have the freedom to make choices. Therefore, you will reap the consequences of the choices you make, whether they are good or bad.

A major reason for divorce is selfishness. Each want their spouse to please them. I want what I want right now! I want a new house. I want a new car. I want another baby. I want more money. I want dinner prepared when I get home from work. I want you to prepare dinner since I work like you do. Each want what they want. However, we learned that love is not selfish. Therefore, we can learn from past mistakes and not commit them in future relationships. Why do you think people get married three or more times? They have not learned from past mistakes. One cannot keep blaming the fifth spouse. There must be a time when we look in the mirror at ourselves. What am I doing wrong? Take personal inventory and be accountable for the part you played in the severing of your marriage. Learn to be the best husband and wife you can be. Learn to walk in forgiveness. Learn not to hold grudges. Learn what it means to walk in love. Learn to be a godly example to your spouse and to your children. As you began to learn and practice these things, you are moving forward in the right direction. Don't allow the past scars and past hurts paralyze you from moving forward in Christ. Enjoy your single life and be open for whatever God has for you in the future. He knows what is best for you! Enjoy the journey with Him by your side.

Review Questions:

1. If you are separated or divorce, why is there still hope for you?

2. What was King David response to his sin with Bathsheba?

3. Why did King David not blame Bathsheba?

4. How should we treat our former spouse?

5. Why does God hate divorce?

6. Why is selfishness one of the major reasons for divorce?

7. How can one learn from past mistakes in a marriage?

Chapter Fourteen

PRE-MARRIAGE COUNSELING SESSIONS

**Where no counsel is, the people fall: but in the
multitude of counselors there is safety.**
Proverbs 11:14

The goal of pre-marriage counseling is to provide a safe place to determine if they are prepared for marriage. A couple does not need counseling to get married. My position is to point out warning signs that could hurt their marriage. Of course, they can ignore the warning signs and get married anyway. However, I will not perform their wedding. I will not do pre-marriage counseling with a couple that has their wedding date, ordered their cake, and sent our invitations. Why would I even counsel them? They are prepared to get married! They booked their honeymoon in advance and will not cancel regardless of the warning signs I see. I do not charge them since I genuinely want to help couples start their marriage on a solid foundation. However, I refuse to waste

my time counseling any couple who has everything set. This is how I feel. Other counsellors may feel differently. That is fine with me. In my years of counseling, I can only remember two couples who promise not to marry if I pointed out severe, danger signs to them. They did not get married, and both couples eventually broke up. I have a job to do and will be true to my convictions. My goal is to help each couple prepare for marriage and to assist in providing a solid foundation for marriage. See, the actual wedding may last for an hour, but the marriage is designed to last a lifetime.

I will share five of my pre-marriage counseling sessions, and five of my marriage counseling sessions. Please understand no names will be given. The Bible says that there is nothing new under the sun. Ecclesiastes 1:9 NIV. The marriage problems in these sessions are not new just manifested in diverse ways in different people. No marriage problem is an isolated event. My pre-marriage sessions span forty years from twelve, different churches and continue still in 2022 without charge. There is not one person who can say that I charge them for my service. I am equally proud to say that not one person ever came back and said that I gave them wrong advice or bad counsel. To God be the glory!

Session I: I was asked to counsel this middle-aged couple. My sessions our for five weeks for two hours each session. This couple was mature and committed to the Lord. They loved each other and was committed to having a strong relationship and marriage. On the first night, I asked them to write ten things they admire in their mate. Let me say here that I was saddened when one partner could only think of two or three things that they admire about the person they plan on marrying. That was not an effective way to start our session. However, this couple did the exercise. Each week we explored a different section in marriage. In week three, I asked them to name one thing that bothers them about their mate. This was an exciting time of heart-felt communication. In week one, I told them to be honest with me throughout these sessions. Tell me the truth! I cannot help you if you are not going to be honest with me. Everything is confidential! They trusted me, and I have not shared their names to anyone. The woman stated that he is a workaholic and needs to spend more quality time with me. We discussed that, and he agreed to do better. The man stated that she doesn't defend me against her adult children. She always takes their side on issues concerning our relationship and upcoming marriage. Her children declared they are not coming to the wedding. I stated to her do not allow anyone to force you to cancel your wedding, not even your children. They have their own life to live and so do you! Just as you want your man to defend you, you must be willing to defend your man also. She understood! The following week she shared that I told my children that I love them, but I love this man also. I would love to have your support, but I am getting married. Her children did not attend the wedding. They are happily married as I share session one with you.

Session II: Some pre-marriage counseling seems like the odd couple, but one cannot prejudge anyone without the facts. While they accepted Christ as their Savior, they were like babes in Christ and needed to grow more. I challenged them to spend more time in the Word of God and attend church regularly. They loved and respected each another. However, I shared a danger sign that may manifest itself in the future. She was a neurosurgeon, and he was a trash collector. I often heard that opposite attracts. Well, I saw it in this relationship. They shared about how they met and their first date. It was very romantic just like yours. They went through each lesson with me, and I drilled them with questions, and they asked me questions also. However, I had one major concern. Because of the differences in their educational background and income, it may become a problem in the future. I told her she must never ridicule her husband for his lack of education. He will be your husband, your protector, and leader in the home. Do not put him down when an argument erupts. He loves you and will do anything for you. Please don't disrespect him because of his educational background. If that is a major problem right now, do not marry him. You know that his funds are limited. Do not destroy him for not making much as you. You must love him for the man that he is and not for the man you want him to become. They married and had two children. After six years of marriage, he left the home due to a major argument. She told him to get a real job. My understanding is he never went back. The scripture tells us that death and life are in the power of the tongue, and they that love it shall it the fruit thereof. Proverbs 18:21. Our negative speech can destroy a marriage and a home. Be careful what you say. We must be swift to hear, slow to speak, and slow to wrath or anger. James 1:19. They have not requested a counseling session together with me.

Session III: This young couple received five weeks of counseling. I poured all I could into them. I loved them and wanted their marriage to succeed. Marriage is not a fairy tale. It is demanding work and built on trust, and the willingness to work things out in difficult times. After several years of marriage, they began to drift apart. He began to work more hours to pay the bills. He felt it was his right to have down time enjoying his hobbies. Of course, his wife felt rejected and alone even though he was paying all the bills. I was able to talk with them. However, it did not go well. He was on the defense, and that was not good. I reinforced to him his role as a husband and her role as a wife. I told them to communicate each day in love. I met with them months later, and they were doing much better. Now, it has been years since I have spoken to them. I pray they are during well since I have not seen them in years.

Session IV: I have learned so much from this couple. We must listen to those who love us. Why would you not listen to sound advice from someone who has your best interest at heart? I wanted this marriage to be successful like all of them. Both professed their commitment to Christ. However, it must be in practice and not lip service. I did not ask them if there were any unhealthy habits they needed to overcome before their marriage. I found out after the wedding that there were gambling and pornography issues from her husband. The gambling issues almost cost them their house. He believed no help was needed for his gambling issues nor for his hunger for pornography. One will not receive help if he believes nothing is wrong. Sin can blind us to the reality of the truth. By this time, I was informed that the marriage was a mess. He had to find his own place to live. Now, it is pressure on the wife to pay the bills. God never intended for a wife to be under so much pressure. I did not meet with this couple. I would have told him to get professional help from these two vices. However, he did not believe they were sinful and that he was not hurting anyone. Well, he was hurting his wife and his entire family. How can something or someone have a hold on us so strong that we refuse to get help to save our marriage and our family? I have seen this repeatedly. I could not help this couple. The wife filed for divorce.

Session Five: Many couples have come prepared to receive advice or counsel before their marriage. It is a breath of fresh air when couples come in with a strong commitment to the Lord and to each other. It helps a lot. It is important to begin a marriage on a solid foundation. I have counseled several interracial couples and performed their wedding as well. The ones that I counseled were mature spiritually and knew what they were getting into. The Bible says that love never fails. 1 Corinthians 13: 8. A marriage does not have to fail because of differences in race or differences in cultural backgrounds. These couples understood their differences and were willing to accept and love each other despite their differences.

It was a joy to share with these couples' principles in the Word of God to assist them in making their marriage and family strong. For five weeks, they had strong dialog with me and asked me tough questions. I stated to one of the couples that everyone will not like seeing you together, even some coworkers or a family member. How would you handle that? They could not control what people like or dislike. It was a good answer! They would allow their love for one another to grow despite how others felt about them. We love the Lord, and we love each other. That is a great combination! We went through our lessons each week geared to strengthen their marriage, so when difficult time comes, they will be able to stand. These couples are all during well! They all stay in touch with me. To God be the glory!

Chapter Fifteen

MARRIAGE COUNSELING SESSIONS

> **Be devoted to one another in love. Honor**
> **one another above yourselves.**
> Romans 12:10 NIV

Session 1: *I have the privilege of counseling people from other churches, some were members while others were church leaders. I am humbled and count it an honor to assist my brothers and my sisters. We are members of the same body. My goal is to strengthen the marriage and the family. That has not changed. I would jokingly tell my friends that they come to me for counseling since I do not charge them. My gifts are not for sale. Every person is different. God has been good to me, and I have no problem for those who charge a fee for their services. It is a joy when two unsaved people come in for counseling and leave with Christ in their hearts. What if they did not have the money to pay and miss God's love for them? My family is blessed, and I take no credit for that!*

When I am asked to counsel members from other churches, my answer is no. I will not counsel anyone from other churches without the permission of their pastor. This has worked well for me, and every pastor gave me permission to counsel their sheep. We must do things right as leaders. As I counseled members from other churches, some had major problems. A marry man had sex with another woman in the church. The lady got pregnant, and it was a mess. My goal was to bring order out of chaos. The first step started with repentance and forgiveness from the heart. The second step was taking responsibility for one's actions by apologizing to the wife and the other woman. The third step was letting his pastor know what has transpired. The Bible teaches that whoever covers his sins will not prosper, but whoever confess and forsake them shall have mercy. Proverbs 28:13 We all need the mercy of God since we all fall short of His glory! I admired this husband and his wife. She stood by her husband and was determined to do what was necessary, so they could move forward in Christ and with their lives. We had tough dialog about the baby and the baby mother. He owned up to his lack of judgment and to his responsibility to do what was right. After we completed our five-week sessions, I called his pastor and told him we were done. He thanked me and said that he would take it from there. I have not heard from this couple but believe they are doing well. God is a restorer, and He will never abandon His children. He is rich in mercy! However, we must do like King David and come clean!

Session II: This couple loved God and served regularly at church in various areas. Do not ever think that because one is saved and love the Lord that a marriage will not ever need help or guidance. It was an honor to impart to them the wisdom the Lord gave me to share. I take no credit for anything! This was many years ago that I met with them, but I remember the things we went over. Because he had a servant heart, he would serve wherever the need was. However, it took time away from his wife. She wanted her husband back. I could relate to that also. My wife did not marry the church, she married me. Therefore, she must be a priority and know with certainty that she is a priority! Children grow up hating church. They would tell me that church took their parents *away from them. Parents must have balance. Some children are failing in school, while the parents are having an exciting time at church. Parents must be involved in the life of their children. We participated in our children's life and not just in academics. They played different sports along with different activities, and each found what they really like. Husbands and wives must grow together. It will not happen if we fail to spend quality time with each other. The wife shared that she could not remember the last time they went on a date or went to a nice place for dinner. It was about being in all the church services each week and especially on Sunday. Thank God for church, but pastors go on vacations! Who is more important than the pastor? I know one pastor who takes a whole month off. What godly wisdom! When we are overworked on the job, overworked at church, and overworked at home, our bodies will break down. You know that's the truth, especially as we get older. I gave the husband an assignment. I told him to take his wife out to a lovely place, not McDonald's or Wendy's but someplace nice and tell me about it in our next session. I can honestly say that she came in our next session with a huge smile on her face. I knew he did something right, and I could not wait to hear it! She shared that they took the train to Virginia to see a play. I can still see her face radiating with joy! Then, she made my heart melt. She said, "Pastor Norman, we missed church on Sunday!" I yelled out, "Praise God!" That was the turning point in their marriage. Every marriage needs a turning point. What turning point is needed in your marriage? After years of marriage, we can lose our passion. Our fire, which was a flame in the beginning is down to a flicker. We forgot why we married in the first place. Bills, children, employment, and yes church work have a way of consuming most of our time. Therefore brothers, we must be wise and take some me time with the wife. I remember we left our three, teenage kids at home while we went to Florida. I told them that dad and mom need a vacation. Do not burn down the house! We knew our kids and trusted them. We had neighbors they could call and relatives nearby. I left them so much food for each day, and money to buy items they wanted. All of them had summer jobs. We enjoyed ourselves in Florida and did not worry about* them. We instilled in them godly principles by our teaching and example before them. This couple is doing great!

Session III: This couple came in for counseling. They had lived together for ten years and had three children and wanted to get married. However, they had issues. Remember, nothing new is under the sun. Both were professional people with great jobs and making a lot of money. They were not working as a team and spent little time together. This couple had a routine that they followed each day. It got to be boring! Yes, they had great sex, but a healthy marriage is more than sex.

I believed in helping people where they are. I did not know them, but they wanted to get married. Why did they wait so long to get married? They could have gone to the Justice of the Peace and got married right away and save a lot of money. My goal is to help people where they are.

Our five sessions would give them tools to have a stronger relationship with the Lord and to follow His teaching. They must make a quality decision to put God first. The fact that they requested counseling is a step in the right direction. It is not my job to make decisions for them. There are debates concerning living together. Each church or each pastor teaches what they believe is right. I know firsthand that many who professed Christ are living together. I share what the Word of God says and leave the rest to them. Jesus shed His blood for them not me. I remember several couples in counseling decided they would not have sex until after they were married even though they were living together. That was a big step! See, God's Word can change the heart. The problem is we throw Christians into deep waters before they learn to swim. We put demands on people without allowing the Holy Spirit to work in their hearts. This couple have been living together for ten years and had three, small children. Now, some teach that one must leave the home to show they are Christians. Listen clearly, a person comes to Christ with a smoking habit. He has been smoking a pack a day for ten years. However, he understood clearly what he needed and accepted Jesus as His Savior. Will the church tell him to leave until he has kicked the smoking habit? The more we feed on the Word of God and learn to yield to the Holy Spirit, He will help us overcome unhealthy habits and personal situations we find ourselves in. I fed this couple the Word of God, so they will be in a better position to make quality decisions on the welfare of their family. They can never come back and say that I gave them wrong advice. This couple is married and still together.

Session IV: This couple lifestyle was a dysfunctional mess! They knew it, and I knew it. I commend them for reaching out for help. There were so many issues such as blended families, mental and physical abuse, poor living conditions, trust issues, infidelity, lack of money, and seven children between the two of them. They all lived together in a small, two-bedroom apartment along with several relatives. I started at the beginning with them to make a commitment to follow Christ. Everything starts with a relationship with Him. Because we chose to follow our own path and desires, our lives will spiral out of control, and we will be on a downward slide until we decide to follow and obey the Lord.

Normally, my counseling sessions are five weeks. Considering their present situation, ten weeks were needed for them. I had to rearrange my schedule several times because of their children needs. I did not know this couple. One of their mistakes was getting married and did not know each other. They got married for the wrong reasons. We began our sessions trying to build on a solid foundation in the Word of God. Both confessed they were Christians. I attacked their problems with practical solutions.. I explained to them that they did not get into this mess overnight, and it will not go away overnight. They must be intentional about following the plans I laid out for them. Remember, nothing is new under the sun. Other couples had some of the same issues just like them. Blended family was an issue. One could not buy ice cream for his children and leave the other children out. If you cannot buy for all, don't buy for one! Give the same correction to all the children that were involved. I suggested they plan and work together to get a bigger apartment. The kids will not be small forever so prepare for that. We had detailed conversations concerning trust and fidelity issues. The good news is they owned up to their mistakes. We address police officers coming to their home for loud screaming and fighting. I explained their actions does not represent

Christ. How can you win a neighbor to the Lord with all that drama? I would not want your Jesus after watching you fight one another. Each of them must strive to be Christ-like. It will not happen overnight, but small victories will turn into big victories. Due to schedule issues, we had to stop our sessions. They have major challenges ahead, but by following godly principles, they can succeed.

It has been years since I have spoken to them.

Session Five: I was surprised that church leaders had titles but no training. It was my responsibility to train and assist them in becoming effective leaders in their church. It is the same way with marriage. Couples get married with little or no training and wonder why their marriage is falling apart. Who would go to have surgery by an untrained surgeon? It would be a lawsuit! Yet, couples get married all the time with little or no training, and some are Christians. Do not expect your marriage to be successful just because you are a Christian. Indeed, that should help. The good news is that Christians can have a failed marriage, divorce, and still go to heaven. Thank God that our salvation is not based on our performance. If it were based on whether we stayed married, many Christians would be in a lot of trouble.

This couple asked me to counsel them. They are leaders in their church but had marital issues. They would argue all the time but faithful in attending church. As we had our first session, I notice that both had strong wills and not afraid to speak up, In some marriage sessions, the wife had no voice. That was not the case here. I encourage the wife to have a voice since she is part of a team. However, her voice should not consistently override the voice of her husband. I don't believe her voice overrode her pastor, so why should her voice override her husband. If you have a good husband, give him the respect that he is due. We went over each role. I discovered that neither had training before they were married. I was able in our five session to give them a foundation of Godly principles that will help their marriage. We cannot assume that just because a couple is a leader in the church or have been married for some time that they received training. I commend this couple for asking for help even though they are leaders in their church. It is no shame to ask for help to save your marriage. This couple has grown spiritually and has grown in their marriage. To God be the Glory!

Extra Session: This young woman requested counseling. She was being abused by her husband. He broke her nose in the past and put a gun up to her head. If he had a bad day, he would come home and take it out on his wife. He was big, and she was petite. In our first session, she asked if she divorces her husband, would God be mad at her? After she told me all that she is going through at home, I told her God wants you safe and secure, and you are not a punching bag. She moved out and her husband came to her church to see her. He was not a church goer. He asked her to come back home, but she refused. He asked her out for dinner, but she refused. He asked her if he could come to her next counseling session. She was not sure. She called me and asked what I thought. I told her if you want him to come that is find with me. He came to our next session, and he was a big man. He started off nice but when I challenged him on why he was physically abusing his wife, he got angry. I told him that a husband hands are there to protect and bring comfort to his wife. Your hands bring hurt, pain, and discomfort. Why should any wife come back to a man that makes her life miserable and caused her to have low self-esteem and lots of pain? He was angry and left. After our five weeks sessions was over, I did not hear from her for about two years. She moved to another state and divorced her husband. She told me life is good. She found a great church, and she got her self-esteem back. She thanked me for assisting her. To God Be the Glory!

All marriages will not end happy ever after. However, like this sister, you can move forward with your life! Apply Godly principles to your life as you move forward. Do not accept mental or physical abuse! You are not chained to that man or that woman. Abuse is wrong no matter where it comes from. I hope you will follow these suggestions!

Chapter Sixteen

CONCLUSION

Let us hear the conclusion of the whole matter; Fear God, and keep His commandments: for this is the whole duty of man.
Ecclesiastes 12:13-14

You have been given godly principles that will enable you to be the husband, wife, father, mother, son, and daughter that God requires. Review this book several times and even highlight certain sentences and paragraphs. The welfare of your marriage and family are at stake. Spend time answering the review questions. Began to practice these godly principles one step at a time. No one reach the top of the mountain by wishing and hoping. It takes yielding to the Holy Spirit and a determination to follow these godly principles. You reach the top of the mountain by taking one step at a time. You may slip but keep moving forward! As you do this, you will grow, and your marriage will be blessed. Your children will be blessed because of your example in Christ. Listen to this, my sister came to Christ at sixteen. We would fight all the time. I remember punching her in the face. She threw a sharp knife at me and cut my arm. When I became a Christian, I did not fight her anymore even when she picked fights with me. She saw me praying and having Bible study with another brother. My sister saw how I changed. She came to church with me and gave her heart to the Lord. My sister and her husband have been copastors for over twenty-five years in Florida. God promise that His Word will always produce fruit. It will accomplish all He wants it to, and it will prosper everywhere He sends it. Isaiah 55:11 NLT. The keys are in your hands. This book is in your hands. Study it and apply its principles. Your marriage and your family will never be the same! I can't save your marriage, but you can!

About Norman Bishop

Norman serves as an Elder and as an assistant pastor of Bethel Deliverance International Church. He serves as pastor of pastoral care making sure every person is cared for. He uses the elders, ministers, and deacons to help fulfill the vision of his Pastor. Norman received his Master's Degree from Liberty University in Pastoral Counseling in 2014. He has been advising and counseling for forty years and continues in 2022. He began teaching at Deliverance Evangelistic Bible Institute in 1978 for twenty years. He also taught children's church and Sunday school. He served as a deacon for ten years.

For the past two years, Norman has conducted zoom classes from diverse topics during the pandemic. He also serves as Bethel home cell pastor making sure each lesson is in line with the preaching and teaching of his pastor. The cell leaders teach the lesson to those who call in. Due to the pandemic, we are not meeting in homes. Norman was given the assignment to train church leaders from twenty-five churches. He serves without fanfare not looking for recognition but want others to be touch by the power of God and by the love of God.

Contact Information

You can contact Pastor Norman through his email address: pohsib1955@gmail.com

Or phone
215-336-2718

Printed in the United States
by Baker & Taylor Publisher Services